O. H. Morgan, E. R. Murphy

History of the 7th Independent Battery

Indiana Light Artillery

O. H. Morgan, E. R. Murphy

History of the 7th Independent Battery
Indiana Light Artillery

ISBN/EAN: 9783337272470

Printed in Europe, USA, Canada, Australia, Japan

Cover: Foto ©Andreas Hilbeck / pixelio.de

More available books at **www.hansebooks.com**

HISTORY

OF THE

7th Independent Battery

INDIANA

∴LIGHT ARTILLERY,∴

—BY—

O. H. MORGAN AND E. R. MURPHY.

WAR OF THE REBELLION,

1861 TO 1865.

PRESS OF THE DEMOCRAT,

1898.

On September 7, 1861, Samuel J. Harris received authority to organize a battery of light artillery, the result being the organization of the Seventh Independent Battery, Indiana Light Artillery, as follows:

Captain, Samuel J. Harris;

1st. Lieutenant, Lewis B. Leonard;

2nd. Lieutenants, George R. Swallow, Otho H. Morgan, John J. Hawes, and Frank W. Buckmar;

1st. Sergeant, Mahlon Johnson;

Q. M. Sergeant, John C. Fislar;

Duty Sergeants, George M. Repp, Albert R. Piper, George K. Huffman and Edgar R. Murphy;

Corporals, Benjamin F. Roberts, D. Newton McKee, Fenton Butterfield, Sterling Carter, Milton Boyd, Jacob W. Harris, Abner Cook, Columbus S. Pound;

Artificers, Lewis J. Ramsey, Jacob F. Rosenbarger, William H. Hartley, and Michael W. Wilson;

Buglers, Audrew M. Carmichael, and John E. Bowman;

Privates, Alex Abbott, James E. Anderson, Newton Bledsoe, John W. Boyd, Robert O. Bosley, John Bush, Charles Brash, Ed H. Cole, William Cutsinger, Joel H. Crum, Elihu Dixon, James Duncan, Edwin S. Dille, John P. Allen. Stephen S. Batt, George W. Bealman, William D. Burch, Landa T. Bryant, Asa D. Broady, John C. Cline, William Coman, John H. Crane, Samuel C. Colebaker, John Duff, George Dunlap, Hugh Daugherty, Thomas J. Fulk, Nathaniel Fish, Isaac Funderburg, Jacob Garris, John Garr, Crispen S. Goen, Robert Gallbraith, William F. Gibson, William H. Hackley, Martin Haggard, John W. Heller, Charles Hickling, James Hord, Mervin Hubbard, Greenburg Huff, Abner E. Haines, Fred Helmohl, George W. Hall, Adam Johnson, Joseph S. Ketcham, John M. Kemp, Israel Ketchem, John W. Kitzmiller, Asa Leach, George F. Long, George L. Lindsey, George W. May,

Cyrus Martin, James H. McCoskey, David C. Mann, Jacob
McConnelly, Edward McIntosh, Solomon McIntosh, James
McKain, Charles May, Abner Mitchem, Nehemiah Mitchen,
Tillman A. Moore, Levi D. Myers, William S. Moore, Thomas
McQuilkin, John F. Martin, George C. Masterson, Ithamer C.
Owens, George Paul, Thomas R. Palmer, Thomas Parsons,
Jackson Petro, Jesse Pound, Abram S. Reel, Andrew Reubright,
Lewis Reubright, John Reynolds, Jasper Reno, Christ Ritline,
William A. Russell, Jason A. Rogers, James A. Risley, Beacham
Rhodes, John Short, John E. Scott, James Smallwood, Joseph
E. Smallwood, George Slusser, Tillman C. Stewart, Henry
Smallwood, Ward Salmond, William H. Spurgeon Henry a
Steinbarger, John Stultz, William A Taylor, Joseph M. Thomp-
son, William A. Thurston, George W. Vancleave, Edgar T.
White, Charles Williams, Theadore Wiles, David A. Welch,
Miles B. Young, which were mustered into the service by Col,
Wood, on the second day of December, 1861. While organizing
the men were rendezvoused at Camp Morton until Nov 20,
1861, when they moved to Camp Frybarger, where they re-
ceived their clothing, guns, horses, and everything to complete
the organization, and left for the seat of war, stopping at Camp
Joe Holt, at Jeffersonville, Indiana, for two days, receiving orders to proceed to Camp Gilbert, four miles east of Louisville,
Kentucky.

On December 18, 1861, the organization was completed by
the assignment of Lewis B. Leonard, George R. Swallow, Otho
H. Morgan and John J. Hawes, all Lieutenants, to their respec-
tive positions. Our camp at this time contained seven batteries, viz: Terrell's regular, twelve guns; Drury's Third Wisconsin, six guns; Stevens' Twenty-sixth Pennsylvania, six guns;
Loomis' Michigan battery, six guns; two Ohio batteries of six
guns each, and the Seventh Indiana, of six guns. These batteries formed an artilley brigade, under command of Capt.
Terrell. Every day when the weather would permit they were
ordered out to gun, battery, or brigade drill.

On Sunday night, December —, 1861, orders were received
to strike tents and take cars to Mumfordsville, reaching that
point on Monday night at twelve o'clock. On Tuesday morning the battery proceeded to Camp Wood, about three miles
from Green river, with about 10,000 troops camped about us.
Here forces are thrown across the river every day to protect

the workmen on the railroad bridge destroyed by Genl. Buckner.
The battery has been assigned to Genl. Mitchell's division, but
to no brigade.

Genl. Buckner is reported ten miles from us in the direction of Bowling Green with a force of ten thounsand confederates. and from preparations going on, an attack is expected.
We have orders, at the sound of firing in the direction of
the river, to harness up and move to the front.

On Thursday, January 29, 1862. an engine and freight train,
collided near our camp and was a complete wreck. By command
of Genl. Terrell, a detail from each battery was made to clear the
road; the men worked one day and night in a drenching rain,
when they were relieved by a force of experts at that business.
Three men were killed by this wreck and three badly wounded.

On Friday, January 13, the body of Genl. Zollicoffer and
Capt. Payton killed in the engagement at Mill Springs, passed
through our camp, enrout to the confederate lines. About noon
the advance of Genl. Mitchell's division from Bacon Creek made
its appearance and passed on towards the river. While camped here we had continual bad weather, but with all this we had
to be out to drill, either brigade, battery or gun.

On February 13, we receceived orders and started in a
drenching rain to go to West Point, at the mouth of Salt river,
on the Ohio river and report to Genl Nelson, and there we were
to take transports to go to the support of Genl. Grant, at Fort
Donaldson. On our first night we reached Bacon Creek, arriving late in the evening, all being tired and wet, went in camp
without putting up teuts, depending upon the gun paulins for
shelter. On Friday morning, the 14th, we found a severe snow
storm had set in, and it was turning bitterly cold; we started on
the march and found the roads almost impassable; we had to
cut roads through the timber and lay down fences and pick our
way the best we could. The seventh and Terrell's battery were
moving together, the five other batteries were following with
Genl. McCook's division. After a march of thirteen miles we
halted for the night and took possession of a church, which
made very comfortable quarters. At sunrise on Saturday the
15th, we were off and had overtaken Genl. Nelson's division,
which was resting by the road. He ordered us into camp and

just as we had pitched tents, orders came to return to our old camp at Green river.

February 16 found us back to Camp Wood, worn out and weary, receiving orders that night to be ready to move at eight o'clock the next morning and proceed by the pike to Bowling Green, Genl. Mitchell having found that place vacated.

On Monday, February 17, we struck tents, and after dark moved across the river on the railroad bridge, and went into camp, where we spent the night by a bright camp fire, without any shelter.   We got along very well until very late in the night, when a hard rain set in and made sleep impossible.   At 4 o'clock a. m , on the 18th, we were on the march.   Seven batteries composed the column of artillery.   We had a terrible march, on account of mud and rain.   The horses would drop in their harness from sheer exhaustion.   The roads had been plowed up, and at places filled with felled trees.   We traveled until 3 o'clock. p m., but only made ten miles.   We went into camp at a beautiful spot, with plenty of forage of every description.   The exposure of that terrible night at Bacon creek had disabled several members of the battery, and the hardships go e through since compelled us to leave some of them at this point.   They were afterward removed to Bowling Green and placed in the hospital.

On Wednesday, February 27, the battery moved to the river opposite Bowling Green.   The river being very high and we having to wait our turn to cross, we were delayed until after dark.   The approach to the crossing was over a low, swampy bottom and a corduroy road, and the night was extremely dark.   All these together made it quite difficult   Going into camp near where we crossed we remained here three days.

On March 1 we started for Nashville, nothing of importance transpiring on the march.   Everything along the line seemed to be deserted except occasionally in passing a cabin the stars and stripes would be waved at us.   We lived off the best there was in the land, camping one night at Tyree Spring, and arriving at Edgefield, opposite Nashville, on March 2, late in the evening, where we again went into camp.   All bridges across the Cumberland river have been destroyed, and the water very high.   We have to wait an opportunity to cross.   The gunboat Cairo is here, her guns bearing on the city.

Nashville was hurriedly evacuated as evidenced by the army supplies. About $1,000,000 worth, left unharmed. The number of batteries here now are 25. On Friday, March 8, the command crossed the river on a transport and went in camp about one mile from the city, the battery was here assigned to Genl. Nelson's division.

Here, through exposure to cold, rain and neglect of proper medical attention, our battery is much reduced by sickness.

· On Thursday, March 13, the battery with two brigades of Nelson's division, with Genl. Nelson and staff, set out to the hermitage, ten miles beyond our picket line. The command was halted in front of Genl. Jackson's old home, the battery fired a salute over the grave of the hero of New Orleans, after which the command return to camp.

The battery was here assigned to the twenty-second brigade, Col. Bruce commanding, it is composed of the first, second and twentieth Kentucky regiments and the seventh Indiana battery.

Wednesday, March 19, everything was in readiness, and at 6 o'clock a. m. were under way with our new division.

Thursday, March 20, found the command thirty-five miles from Nashville, awaiting the completion of a bridge. While at this point we were frequently called out, but in every case these calls proved to be false alarms.

Having lost quite a number of men by sickness, a detail was made today (Friday, March 21,) from the infantry, to fill the required number in the battery. On Sunday, March 23, Capt. S. J. Harris tendered his resignation as captain of the battery—an act which was much regretted by the company. Today the battery passed through Columbia, and camped upon the plantation of Confederate General Pillow. His residence was made headquarters.

A few miles south of the Pillow place the army passed the home of Gen. Polk. In a march of fifteen miles we struck a rough, barren country, and here, among the poorer class, we found a strong Union sentiment. At the little village of Waynsboro the northern soldier was welcomed, and when the band struck up "Columbia" the people broke into cheers. The ladies waved their handkerchiefs, and a large American flag was brought forth and spread to the breeze, which the boys all cheered as they marched by. Five men followed us into camp and were mustered into the service and became members of the battery.

On Friday, March 28, the battery received orders to be ready to move at 8 o'clock the next morning, with five days' rations. Moving on toward Pittsburg Landing the afternoon of April 5 found the battery at Savannah, and camped near the river. The next morning the command was ordered to be ready to move, and laid in waiting to be transported across the river. For the lack of means for transporting troops across, the order was countermanded.

Monday noon the battery was loaded on a transport and ferried across the river, and by the time it was unloaded it was dark. The battery camped upon the battlefield for the night, and when the men were routed out in the morning they found the dead lying thick around them. The battery camped here until the advance on Corinth.

May 1 found the command yet at Pittsburg Landing, with the advance on the road to Corinth, five miles to the front. The Captain has orders to move up to the front in the morning. prepared with seven days' rations. During our stay here the battery was transferred to the twenty first division, Genl. T. L. Crittendea commanding.

Mry 16 finds us near Corinth. During the time between May 1 and 16, Capt. Harris having left, and Lieut. L. B. Leon· ard resigned, an officer from a Michigan battery had been put in command, to the great dissatisfaction of the officers and men. While laying in camp Genl. Nelson gave his command plenty of exercise by having them out at all times of the night fighting some imaginary foe.

Tuesday afternoon, May 20, a heavy attack was made by our right wing, Generals Pope and Buell advancing their whole force, crossing the swamp in their front, and driving the enemy's pickets. The whole line was then advanced, and now and then the enemy would bring out a battery, but they were soon silenced. The whole line was advanced some every day.

Friday, May 23, finds Gov. O. P. Morton, the War Governor of Indiana, with us, and Lieut. Swallow determined to get rid of our Michigan Captain. He presented the case to the Governor, who said he would dispose of the Michigan gentle-

man, and immediately wrote the appointment of Lieut. George
R. Swallow as Captain, and Lieut. Otho H. Morgan as Senior
First Lieutenant. Here the battery was reduced to four guns,
the Michigan Captain taking with him two guns. One section
of the battery was on picket duty today, and as it rained hard
they had everything but a pleasant time.

' Monday, May 26, found us yet in line, and Tuesday a general advance was made, the Confederate pickets retiring, contesting stubbornly every foot of ground. Genl. Crittenden
gave consent to open on where we judged the enemy were, and
we sent a shower of shell through the woods in the direction of
Corinth, at a range of about one mile. Although the only way
we could locate the enemy was by the noise of their drums, yet
the skirmishers report that every shell exploded inside their
lines. The enemy did a great deal of cheering and we could
hear the cars running all night. It was expected we would
hear the next morning of the enemy being reinforced, but about
six o'clock a. m. a dense cloud of smoke and heavy explosions
in the vicinity of Corinth announced that they were vacating.

Remaining about Corinth until the ninth of June, when
we left a fine camp and all in excellent health, the command
marched to East Port, where we remained until the 11th, when
the march was made to Iuka, thence to Tuscumbia and on to
Florence, which place was reached the night of the 16th of
June. An artillery reserve has been formed, of which the battery is a part, but we move the greater part of the time with
the twenty-first division. Our marches have been very severe
owing to the extreme heat. We start early in the morning,
resting in the heat of the day, and moving on in the cool of the
evening. As soon as Genl. McCook crossed the river from Tuscumbia we followed, remaining at Florence until the 26th, about
sundown, when we moved along until two o'clock the next
morning, when we laid by for about one hour, when we moved
on to within fourteen miles of Athens and went into camp.
Monday morning, June 30, the command marched through
Athens, and camped within three miles of the town. The
three divisions and their batteries spent the fourth day of July
1862, here awaiting the repairing of the railroad between us
and Nashville. Nelson's, Wood's, and Crittenden's divisions
are here, while McCook's and Mitchell's are at Huntsville.

On July 11 Lieut. Buckmar received orders detailing him to go north and recruit men for the battery.

July 26 found us at Huntsville, and on half rations. On the afternoon of the 28th one of Genl. Buell's staff held a review of the eight batteries camped here.

August 17 found us at Decard Station, and Lieut. Morgan, who had been acting quarter master for the artillery brigade, was released and transferred back to the battery. The troops have built a fort which we occupied on August 25, from which we can command the buildings containing supplies. A general move of troops took place today; Sergt. C. S. Pounds returned from the north with fourteen recruits.

On the fifth day of September we found all forces and wagon trains gone, nothing left except the seventh battery and its support, under command of Genl. W. L Smith. Finally we had orders to move, taking the road leading paralel to the railroad burning bridges and destroying everything that would be of benefit to the enemy, marching the first day to Tullahoma and camping there at night, moving next morning and taking a road to the east of the railroad, passing through a very rough and hilly country, often having to clear the road that we might pass. On this march we captured several horses and had a good time in general, arriving at Murfreesboro in the evening and camping there at night, proceeding next day to Nashville, arriving there on Sunday, September 7. We were rear guard for Buell's army from Decard Station to Nashville.

Lieut. O. H. Morgan left Nashville on Monday evening, September 9, with his section and reported to Col. Woolford, who with his cavalry was guarding a train of supply wagons. Capt. Swallow followed with the remainder of the battery and two companies of the ninth Michigan regiment and left the pike to the right at Edgefield Junction, going probably three miles, for the purpose of guarding the road from any attack that might be attempted from that source. While out on this road the artillery had to do videt duty. Here we found a supply store for rebel bushwackers, which was destroyed. Next morning we retraced our steps and took the road toward Louisville, Ky. While ascending the hill at Tyree Spring some mounted men were seen, when all that were mounted in our command made a charge, the enemy disappearing, we moved on and passed the house and come in position in an open field, our support of infantry deployed as skirmishes, we shelled the woods in our front, wounding several. This little fight lasted until dark, when we were greatly relieved by the appearance of Genl. Van Cleave and command, the General sending out quite a heavy line. Early next morning it was discovered that our firing had not been fruitless, that several wounded confederates were found in an old house, we having one man, Chas. Hickling, wounded. Capt. Swallow was here put under arrest for bringing on the engagement, but soon released. We camped here over night, and did not advance until late next day, when the march was resumed, passing through Franklin and Bowling Green, arriving at Cave City on the evening of Monday, September 16, remaining here with a large army, while the Confederates were fighting our men at Mumfordsville. After Bragg's army had crossed the river we were allowed to advance, arriving at the river and finding it very low we had no difficulty in crossing. The battery, with a brigade of cavalry being in advance, we came up with the rear guard of Bragg's army at Vinegar Hill, near Elizabethtown. The cavalry made a charge and received a volley from a masked battery, and retired.   One of the guns of the battery was brought in position when a confederate officer made his appearance in the pike.   The gun was sighted and fired, killing the horse and officer.   The confederates retired, giving us no more trouble, and leaving the road clear for the army to the Ohio river.   The army arrived and went into camp at West Point, at the junction of Salt river and the Ohio river, on the twenty-sixth day of September.   After a pleasant night's rest the march was resumed, and September 28 found the battery camped on Eighteenth street, in Louisville, Ky.

The march from Deckard to Louisville was one mixed with hardship and pleasure, the weather being hot and dry, and water exceedingly scarce, and rations short.   Instead of hardtack flour was issued, and the difficulty of making bread on the march put the soldiers to their wits to invent some way to use it.

When the army left Nashville for Pittsburg Landing all the sick then in camp were either sent home or to a hospital. There were eight of these put aboard the steamer Atlantic. and sent to their homes, by order of Gen. Nelson.   Also on the march those who were not able to move with the battery were left at hospitals, and finally worked their way to Louisville.

On the 10th of July, 1862, the writer of this being one of the party sent home by Col. Nelson, being convalescent, reported to Capt. Fry, in command at Louisville. Ky., and was given seven men, John W. Heller, of the seventh battery, being one of the number. The squad was sent to Camp Gilbert, where the Thirteenth Indiana battery was in camp, and reported to the Captain, who kept us over night and furnished us with clothing. The next day I received orders to take my squad and go to Frankfort and report to Col. Tempel. We arrived at Frankfort the evening of July 11, and were given a small piece of artillery that had to be primed and touched off with a hot iron, so you see we were finely fixed to protect Frankfort from being raided by John Morgan. We spent our time here very pleasantly, being fed by the citizens and treated with the kindest respect. We lived this way until the last week in August, when Gen. Manson came to Frankfort with a new regiment, when I obtained transportation from him for the squad to Louisville. We proceeded then on to the front, stopping over night at Nashville, then on to Deckard. where we found the army in camp.

On the — day of September the battery, with the Twenty-first and Eighth Kentucky, the Fifty first Ohio and the Thirty-fifth Indiana regiments forming Col. Stanley Mathews' brigade of Van Cleve's division of the twenty first corps, Genl. T. L. Crittenden commanding, left Louisville via the Bardstown pike. The command had not gone far when they struck Bragg's outposts, driving them in. From here we were continually fighting the rear guard of the retreating army. At Perryville on October 8, Bragg made a stand. Our division was allowed to remain in seeing distance of that terrible battle, but not allowed to fire a gun. The division camped over night near the battle-field. The next morning we followed the enemy through Perryville and on to Danville. After passing the last named place we discovered a wagon train crossing our road. The battery was placed in position and a few shots fired, and the cavalry was in line, ready for a charge. when all our hopes were blasted by an order from Genl. Buell. That wagon train, like Bragg's army, was permitted to slip our grasp and get out of Kentucky with its booty. We advanced on through Stanford and Crab Orchard. When near the latter place we shelled the retreating

enemy, driving them from a bridge they were trying to destroy,
when the Thirty-fifth Indiana regiment made a charge and
saved the bridge. At this point some members of the battery
captured two of the enemy. We passed on through Crab Orchard, camping near by for the night. The next day the command moved on through Mt. Vernon, London, and on to Somerset, where we went into camp. The night here will not be
forgotten by the officers or men, as it turned bitterly cold and a
severe snow storm set in, and a high wind leveled every tent in
the camp From Somerset our division marched to Columbia,
arriving there on the morning of October 18.   Here, on dress
parade in the evening, order No. 1 was read, announcing the
removal of Genl. Buell, and the appointment of Genl. Rosecrans
to the command of the army of the Cumberland.   No better
news could have been conveyed to the army.

The evening of October 19 finds us camped at Glasgow, Ky.,
where we remained until Monday, Nov. 4, when we left for
Gallatin, Tenn.

Wednesday, Nov. 6, the command is comfortably housed in
Gallatin. The battery, with the Nineteenth Ohio regiment is
to do garrison duty here. Our cannon look frowningly down
four streets entering the town. John Morgan and his forces
were within four miles of us this morning, and captured some
wagons. The command remained here about two weeks, then
moved to Nashville. While camped here the outposts were
often attacked at night, when the battery would be called out
and have to remain with the reserve pickets the remainder of
the night.   :

On the 9th of December the battery, with the twenty-third
brigade, Genl. Stanley Matthews commanding, escorted a train
of wagons on a foraging expedition. They moved out the Murfreesboro pike, almost to Lavergne, turning to the east of the
pike, going to Dobbins' ford, on Stone river. While the wagons were being loaded with corn and what else could be found
that would be of benefit, a division of the enemy came upon the
command and endeavored to cut them off from Nashville, but
failed. The Thirty-fifth Indiana battery did good work in sav-
ing the train. The Major of the Thirty-fifth Indiana regiment
was killed; their Colonel was wounded in the arm; a Captain
of the Fifty-first Ohio regiment was killed; the Union loss in

killed and wounded was about thirty. Information obtained from prisoners taken was that the enemy's force consisted of six regiments and one battery. Two guns of their battery were disabled, and they sustained a loss of one hundred, killed and wounded. The train was safely escorted into Nashville.

On the twenty-sixth day of December the army moved to the front, striking the enemy in force, and our division was brought to a standstill at Lavergne, but the enemy's artillery was soon silenced. On December 29 the army advanced on to Stewart's creek, meeting some resistance but not very strong until within about three miles of Murfreesboro, when on December 30 the enemy opened fire and stubbornly contested every foot of ground. The following was read to the army on the morning of December 31:

"HEADQUARTERS, ARMY OF THE CUMBERLAND,
IN FRONT OF MURFREESBORO, Dec. 31, '62.

General order.

The General commanding desires to say to the soldiers of the Army of the Cumberland that he was well pleased with their conduct yesterday. It was all he could have wished for. He never saw or heard of any skulking. They behaved with the coolness of veterans. He now feels perfectly confident, with God's grace and their help, of striking this day a blow for the country, the most crushing, perhaps, which the rebellion has yet sustained. Soldiers, the eyes of the nation are upon you; the very fate of the nation may be said to hang on the issue of this day's battle. Be true, then, to yourselves; true to your own manly character and soldierly reputation; true to the love of your dear ones at home, whose prayers ascend this day to God for success; be cool; I need not ask you to be brave; keep ranks; do not throw away your fire; fire slow and deliberately; above all, fire low and be always sure of your aim; close steadily in upon the enemy, and when you get within charging distance of the enemy, rush upon them with the bayonet. Do this and the victory will surely be yours. Recollect that there are hardly any troops in the world that will stand the bayonet charge; that those who make it, therefore, are sure to win.

W. S. ROSECRANS,
General commanding Army of the Cumberland."

About 8 o'clock a. m. the battery, with the division, started to cross Stone river. Intelligence was recived that the right was falling back. Col. Fyffe's brigade was ordered to countermarch, and move at double-quick to the right The battery operated for a time with this brigade, shelling the enemy's cavalry from the brick hospital, to the right and rear of the army.

From here the battery with the brigade advanced on the right. The battery took position in a cotton field and shelled the woods, while the infantry advanced to the left oblique, through the field and into the timber. They, having got under cover of the timber and out of the field, a force of the enemy in our immediate front raised and gave us a volley. We, replying with double charges of canister, held our ground until compelled to retire by being completely flanked to our right. An extract from Genl. H. P. VanCleve's report speaks for itself:

"The Seventh Indiana battery, Capt. George R. Swallow, joined us on this open field, and rendered efficient aid. Here I received information from Genl. Rosecrans that Genl. Rousseau was driving the enemy, accompanied with an order for me to press them hard. At the same time I was notified by a messenger from Col. Harker, whose brigade was at my right and rear, that the enemy was in force on my right in a wood, and were planting a battery there. I immediately sent messages to Col. Harker and Capt. Swallow, who was doing good service with his battery, not to suffer it to be captured. The enemy now poured a galling fire of musketry, accompanied by grape and shell. On our right Col. Fyffe's brigade, supported by Capt. Swallow's battery, gallantly returned the fire, but being overpowered by numbers on front and flank, were compelled to retire, followed but a short distance by the enemy. Capt. Swallow, to whom too much praise can not be awarded, brought off his battery safely. I cannot close this report without inviting your attention to the gallantry displayed by those under my command during this engagement. To both officers and men too much praise cannot be awarded. I would particularly notice the coolness, intrepidity and skill of my brigade commanders, Cols. Beatty and Fyffe, and of Capt. Swallow, Chief of Artillery."

In this fight the battery lost Lieut. Buckmar, killed; Smallwood and Munwarren, wounded; George W. Van Cleve, wounded and captured.

From this point the battery was sent to the front and centre to relieve Batteries H and M of the Fourth U. S. artillery and took a position, the left of the battery resting on the Nashville and Murfreesboro pike. Here we did considerable firing and repelled several charges. In his report Capt. Mendenhall, Chief of Artillery of the Army of the Cumberland, says of Batteries H and M and the Seventh Indiana:

"These batteries did much to repel the enemy as they advanced, with the evident determination to drive us back at all hazards, if possible."

Here the battery lost Elihu Dixon and Murdock McGregor, killed.

Moving from here to the left centre and coming in position, there was quite an artillery duel between the Seventh and the celebrated Washington battery of New Orleans. Other batteries had been here before, but were run out. The shell fell fast and thick among us, but we finally crippled and silenced the battery. Withdrawing from here late in the evening and replenishing our caissons with fresh amunition we received orders to take a position on the left and near the river. The battery remained here during the night, it being very cold and wet and rations short. We took in the neighbor's cow and spent the night in roasting beef, along with some of the generals, by a smothered fire. We were tired, wornout and hungry and no one cared to sleep that night.

During the night and morning the whole Union army was massed in a little valley to our rear.

January 2d everything was quiet during the day until about 4 o'clock p. m., when the enemy, under Genl. Breckenridge, advanced driving Col. Beatty, who was on the east side of the river. The enemy advanced to the river and a force came in our immediate front, but they could not withstand the terrible fire of that mass of artillery. They faltered and the infantry with one bound charged and drove the enemy beyond Murfreesboro. During this action fifty-four pieces of artillery were in action.

In this battle the battery lost in killed five, wounded seven. This was a hotly contested battle on both sides and the seventh Indiana battery can proudly claim her share of its honor.

The battery remained on the battlefield until the fifth of
January, when it moved across the river and went into camp
near Murfreesboro. The weather continues the same as when
the army started from Nashville—cold and rainy. Here the
battery put in the time preparing good and comfortoble quarters. Nothing transpired except the regular routine of camp
duty, and being ordered to be ready to move at a moment's notice, and after waiting an hour or two would be ordered back
in camp. Such orders were frequent. some caused by the enemy's cavalry driving in our outposts. At one time a force of
cavalry, and the twenty third brigade, with two sections of the
battery were ordered out on a scout and went about five miles,
when they ran upon a camp of the enemy's cavalry. The party
went into camp and remained until three o'clock a. m., of the
second morning, then breaking camp and returning to Murfreesboro.

On February 14 one section of the battery was sent to a
ford on Stone river, about five miles from Murfreesboro, to do
picket duty. A stockade had been built for us.

Sunday, February 22, Genl. Rosecrans issued an appeal to
the army, asking them that out of respect for the memory of
Washington, whose illustrious virtues we revere, whose wisdom,
justice, and self sacrificing devotion we resolve to imitate ourselves. and teach our children to today renew to each other the
assurance already given of our past toils and sufferings, and
which many of our brave companions have already sealed with
their blood; that we transmit the freedom we inherited from
Washington, unimpaired, to the posterity of our nation—one
and indivisable, or we all perish in its defense.

At sundown the battery took a position in front of headquarters and fired a salute in honor of Washington.

On February 26 an election was held for the selection of a
Second Lieutenant. resulting in the election of Sergt. George
M. Repp.

On February 28 the battery was inspected by Capt. Wood,
who complimented the officers and men for their good appearance.

At every opportunity, when the weather would admit, the
battery was out to drill, as was the case on March 2. On the
fourth day of March Lieut. Repp was sent out with one section

to relieve the section on out post duty at the ford on Stone river. At noon of March 9 the twenty-third brigade, with two guns of the battery, moved out the Shelbyville pike and halted about two miles beyond the pickets of our army. Two of our guns commanded the pike Early the next morning the force formed a line of battle and remained in that position until daylight. During the night a heavy rain set in, which made it very unpleasant. The force remained here until the night of March 10 at 9 o'clock, when orders were received to move immediately, and after marching until two o'clock in the morning we again took possession of our old camp, which had been confiscated by the teamsters.

On March 18, at noon, the battery was on review before Genl. Rosecrans. March 22 Lieut. Morgan, who had been at Nashville, returned with two guns for the battery, making the Seventh a six gun battery. Not having a sufficient number of men a detail was made from the infantry on the 25th.

At noon on the 30th of March the battery moved its camp one mile to the front. On Thursday, April 4 four guns of the battery, with five days' rations, started with Col. Matthew's brigade and several regiments of cavalry, the whole under command of Genl. Stanley. The first day we marched eighteen miles toward Liberty, (or Snow Hill gap), and at five o'clock halted for the night. About midnight we were ordered out, and marched until nearly daylight, when we struck the enemy's pickets. We halted until dawn, when the force began to drive the enemy, and soon found Genl. Morgan's command of confederate cavalry in a strong position. They opened on us with their artillery, but did not accomplish much owing to the distance. The battery was placed in position, and gave them a few rounds, when they moved off through the gap, with our cavalry after them, who report good effect from the battery's firing.

The inhabitants through this section of Tennessee were strongly Union, but were continually harrassed by Confederate cavalry and scouting parties. We camped here over night, when the army moved on toward Lebanon. From the refugees who were with us we learned who were the disloyal citizens along the route, and, by authority of the commanding General, Lieut. Morgan, with a squad of six, went in advance for the

purpose of collecting all the horses and mules he could find.
After scouring the country they met the main force at Lebanon,
about noon. Col. Wilder passed through here yesterday, and
two of his men who had straggled had been shot. One we
found dead and the other was living, but terribly mangled, having been shot three times. Several arrests were made. Along
the road we found the body of a Union man who had been hung
and had his tongue cut out. Two of our own party came near
being captured. They were only saved by the timely notice of
a colored lady that the Confederate cavalry were coming. They
barely had time to mount their horses before the enemy were
onto them. We reached our camp at Murfreesboro on the evening of April 7.   Lieut. Fislar relieved Lieut. Repp's section
from out-post duty on Stone river on May 4. On May 16 Maj.
Mendenhall drilled the three batteries of our division at four
o'clock a. m.

May 23 Lieut. Morgan with his section relieved Lieut.
Fislar at Stone river.

June 2 the Seventh battery was relieved from out-post duty
at Stone river, and Lieut. Morgan called in. June 8 is a day
to be remembered by all troops camped in and about Murfreesboro, as they were all marched up to witness the execution of
Private Hall, of the 59th Ohio infantry.

On June 15 the battery and men were inspected by Capt.
Drewry.

Early in the morning of June 16 the battery was out to
drill, and at nine o'clock the battery, with the whole division,
moved out to witness the execution of a member of the Ninth
Kentucky regiment, who had been tried and convicted for de-
sertion and other offences, and sentenced to be shot.

We remained in camp until Sunday, June 24, when the
army started in a pelting rain on the Chattanooga campaign.
The battery moved into a fort to do garrison duty, and remained there until June 28. At four o'clock that evening the
battery moved out on the Manchester road, divided into sections,
one in front, one in the middle and one in the rear of a train of
about four hundred wagons, loaded principally with ammunition. On June 29 the train was on the march early. It was
still raining, making the roads very bad to travel. Monday
June 30, the train, after a very hard days march, reached the

river, opposite Manchester. On this march the teams and men had a very hard time, the roads being very muddy and cut up. The teams and wagons would mire, and those that could not be started would be burned. Oftentimes we would not get into camp until midnight.

At Beech Gap the advance had quite a battle with the enemy's cavalry. Quite a number were killed and wounded. Tuesday, July 1, the battery crossed the river and camped near town. At dark Lieut. Morgan's section was ordered to the opposite side of the town to guard the railroad bridge. On July 5 Sergt. C. S. Pound received his commission as Second Lieutenant. July 8, in pursuance of orders, the battery fired a salute in honor of the victories of the Union armies, "the fall of Vicksburg and the defeat of Lee." The battery broke camp, and after marching nine miles toward McMinville, camped for the night. McMinville was reached at four o'clock, p. m , July 9. At four o'clock, p. m. on July 20, a volunteer squad, of which Capt. Swallow and Lieut. Morgan, of the Seventh battery, were parties, all under command of Col. Jarvis, went out the Chattanooga road on a scout. They spent the night in climbing the mountain, in a drenching rain, and at daylight dashed into Bushaby Spring, expecting to capture some confederate officers but were disappointed. They returned to camp on the afternoon of the 21st. July 22 sixty men, selected from the three batteries, all under command of Capt. Drwery, of the Third Wisconsin battery, started on a raid through Sequatchee valley where they expected to find a wagon train and lot of camp equippage belonging to John Morgan's command, who is making a raid north of the Ohio river. On the first day they crossed the Cumberland mountain. After dark they decended the mountain into the valley, each man leading his horse down a narrow trail. They halted in front of a cabin at the foot of the mountain, and the scout (a citizen named Jim Smith) opened the couversation with an old lady as follows:

"Well, old lady, are you acquainted with Jim Smith, and do you know where he is?"

"Yes, I know him, but have not seen him for some time."

"Did he not stay here a few nights ago?"

"No. I told you I have not seen him for some time."

Jim walked up to where she could get a good view of him,

and she at once recognized him. Throwing her arms around
his neck she said, "You have come at last, and brought our
brave defenders with you." Her husband ran out of the house
and gave him a hearty slap on the back to testify his delight.
The old lady went to the back of the house after her two sons
who had fled at their approach. The old lady was almost be-
side herself, and about all she could say was "Glory be to God:
my prayers are at last answered and I can again look upon the
old flag." That night the party searched a conscripting officer's house, expecting to find arms, but were disappointed. The
next morning they started on their raid up the valley where no
Union forces had been. They stopped at a Mr. Pope's, and
learned he was an excellent rebel. Breakfast was ordered for
the squad. They entered Pikeville on the afternoon of the
second day out and found that the wagons they had expected
to capture had been taken south some days before.

Just beyond the town they captured eight confederates who
were guarding a lot of cattle. On the afternoon of the third
day they dashed into Sparta and captured a Confederate Quartermaster and took from him eight thousand dollars in Confederate scrip. After a ride of one hundred and sixty miles they
reached camp on the afternoon of the fourth day, bringing
with them a lot of horses and prisoners.

On August 4 Capt. Swallow, with one section of the battery and a force of cavalry and infantry, went on a scout in the
direction of Sparta, returning on the fifth.

On Sunday, August 16, in pursuance of orders, the battery,
with the division, (the Twenty first) broke camp and started in
the direction of east Tennessee. After a march of six miles
they stopped for the night at the foot of the mountain. On the
morning of the 17th reveille sounded at 2:30 o'clock, but it was
fully 8 o'clock before they were on the march. The command
reached the top of the mountain and moved on four miles and
went into camp At 5 o'clock a. m of the 19th, they moved on
and entered Pikeville, in Sequatchee valley, at 4 o'clock. p. m.
While rendezvoused here parties were sent out at different
times, scouting through the country. At one time the division
with its three batteries, crossed the mountain in the direction
of Chattanooga, going within a few miles of that city, accom-
panying a Union Tennessee Colonel to his home, and finding

Confederate pickets on his farm. They returned to Pikeville
the next day, where they remained until Tuesday, Sept. 1. The
march was then taken up at 7 o'clock, and at 4 o'clock went in
camp on the farm of a Mr. Pope, fourteen miles from Pikeville.
Sept. 2 they moved on to within twelve miles of Jasper. Sept.
3 they started at daylight and entered Jasper early in the afternoon, when they went into camp. Sept. 4 they started for
Shell Mound, sending the wagons by way of Bridgeport. The
battery spent the forenoon crossing the Tennessee river, and
camped near the mouth of Nickajack cave. On Sept. 5 the
command did not move until 4 o'clock p. m , and went but a
short distance. On Sept. 6 a march of three miles was made.
Heavy cannonading was heard in the distance. On Sept. 8 the
command moved at daylight and halted after a few miles march.
The twenty-first division, with its three batteries, have reached
Lookout valley, and Sept. 9, while on the march, reports came
that Chattanooga was evacuated, and the command was ordered
to pursue Bragg's army. The command passed over the point
of Lookout mountain in the afternoon, leaving Chattanooga to
our left. We moved on to Rossville. Sept. 10 the advance
was skirmishing with the Confederate rear guard all day, so
they have moved only about eight miles. Sept. 11 the battery
and third brigade was in the advance, and when within three
miles of Ringgold they encountered the Confederate cavalry,
and for a time there was very heavy firing. Four of the battery's guns were brought into action to drive the enemy through
Ringgold and Pigeon Gap, which was successfully done. The
forces followed for three miles beyond the town, where they
went into camp. On the 12 the forces marched back to Ringgold and took a position with the rear guard and moved on to
Lee & Gordon's mill. On Sunday morning, Sept 13, orders came
to send all baggage that would be of any cumbrance to the battery
to the rear, and the division and batteries moved forward in
line of battle, but soon found that the force in our front was but
the rear guard of Bragg's retreating army.

    September 14 we changed camp to Crawfish Spring, three
miles distant, where Genl· Rosecrans had established his headquarters. On September 16 and 17 the troops were annoyed by
frequent dashes of cavalry, and while at dinner on the 18th a
few shells were unceremoniously dropped in the camp. Tents
were immediately struck and the whole army was soon on the

move, one section of the battery going with the cavalry to guard
a ford on the river, near Lee & Gordon's mill, while the rest of
the battery went on some distance farther, and, about 2 o'clock,
p. m., took a position and shelled the woods in advance of the
cavalry. There was nothing more than sharp skirmishing in
our immediate front. Wilder's and Minty's cavalry forces had
been fighting all day on the left. We stopped over night at
this point, and as all blankets and baggage had been sent to
the rear, the officers and men missed them very much, as the
night was very cool and no fires were allowed. All night long
the tramp of Genl. Thomas' corps was heard as they passed on
to the left. After daylight on the morning of the nineteenth
everything was quiet until about 9 o'clock, when the battle
opened on the left, and for five hours the musketry was incess-
ant. About 3 o'clock, p. m., the battery received orders to
move to the left, as the Union forces were giving away. The
battery was mounted and the move made on the gallop, arriving
at the point where needed, and advanced into the timber following the infantry. Soon finding that the battery could be of no
benefit, and was in great danger of being captured, it fell back
across the road into what is known as the Brotherton field.
Here the section that was left at Lee & Gordon's mill met the
other sections and all took position together. The Nineteenth
Indiana, Twenty sixth Pennsylvania, and Third Wisconsin batteries, and four other guns joined in the field, These guns were
hardly in position when the infantry began to fall back. The
guns were double-charged with canister, and held the fire until
the infantry had formed in the rear, and the enemy showed at
the edge of the timber, which was about thirty yards from us.
Orders were given to fire, and immediately 28 guns opened
with terrible effect on the advancing foe. Three times they fell
back, reformed, and charged, but no line of battle could breast
the storm of shot that poured into them. The enemy discovered
that the right flank was unprotected, and, under cover of the
thick timber, threw their forces in that direction. The Union
right being completely flanked the battery was compelled to
fall back at a lively gait, with the loss of one horse killed and
one man wounded. The battery, with the infantry, fell back a
short distance, where a new line was formed, not going in action during the remainder of the day.

Sunday morning, September 20, dawned bright and beautiful. The lines were reformed early, and advanced, opening the fight at 8 o'clock. The battery's position was on a hill west of the Dyer House, as also the two batteries belonging to the twenty first division. The infantry supporting these batteries was ordered forward as reinforcement, and for three hours the artillerymen could look from their high position down on the woods, where the fight was raging fiercely. Everything indicating that the enemy was massing a force for a grand charge. Presently stragglers appeared Then came the forces, slowly yielding but contesting every inch of ground. Then the three batteries, the Twenty-sixth Pennsylvania, Third Wisconsin and Seventh Indiana, opened fire over the columns of infantry. The infantry would form and charge the enemy, then fall back. Everytime the artillery would belch forth the infantry would rally and charge forward, amid the cheers of the battery boys. A gap appearing in the Union line was at once taken advantage of by the enemy, who swept down upon the artillery and were thick among them before they knew it, resulting in the killing of Capt. Stevens, of the Twenty sixth Pennsylvania battery, and the capture of five of his guns. Also the capture of four guns of the Third Wisconsin battery. The battery received orders to limber up and fall back, which was successfully done, with the exception of the right gun, which was run against a stump and had to be left in the hands of the enemy. In this engagement the battery lost in prisoners Lieut. John W. Fislar, Sergt. J. W. Kitzmiller and George W. Slusser. When the firing was first heard in the Twenty sixth Pennsylvania Capt. Swallow rapidly rode up to ascertain the cause, and seeing a man shooting into the battery, advanced toward him saying: "What are you shooting into our own men for?" not knowing his mistake until five guns were pointed at him, with orders to surrender. Leaning on the opposite side of his horse he sang out, "Not much," and came dashing down by the Seventh, crying out, "Limber up and get out of here." The forces fell back across a ravine and into the woods and took a position by the side of the road, where a line was formed. The wagon train was in a valley near by, and would have to pass on this road, therefore it was very important that this point should be well guarded. As soon as it was seen that the right wing of the army was in great peril, the battery's Quartermaster Sergt.

D. Newton McKee, with the blacksmith Newton Bledson, re-
paired with all haste to start the train. After everything had
passed the battery fell in, and proceeded on to Rossville, where
we camped for the night. The next morning we retired to
Chattanooga, and at once began fortifying. September 23
found the forces strongly fortified, while the enemy occupied
Mission Ridge and Lookout Mountain.

Report of CAPT. GEORGE R. SWALLOW, }
Seventh Indiana Battery, Sept., 1863. }

About 12 o'clock, m., 18th inst , the battery received orders to march immediately with the division, to Lee & Gordon's
mills, where they bivouacked for the night.

Saturday, 19th inst., one section was placed in position on
a commanding knoll, and fired a few shells at a gun the enemy
was placing in position on the east bank of the river. This
section was detached, and remained with the third brigade the
remainder of the day. The remaining four guns were ordered
to the front with the second brigade. Took position several
times on the right of the road leading from Lee & Gordon's
mills to Chattanooga, but could do no firing, and seeing part of
our line falling back I retired, and took position on the left of
the road in a small field. Had been in position but a short
time when our line fell back to and across the road. I then
opened upon the enemy a rapid fire with canister, and kept it
up until two regiments fell back through the battery in confusion and disorder. My canister being exhausted and the enemy
in force in front and on the right, I, with some difficulty. withdrew the battery to the rear, and soon after bivouacked for the
night.

Sunday, September 20, took position with two brigades of
our division. They soon advanced to the front, and the battery
advanced to a position in an open field, where we remained a
short time, and were ordered by Major Mendenhall to move to
the left, and when upon a high ridge halted for further orders,
taking a position on the ridge, a little retired. The enemy had
now opened a heavy fire of musketry in our front. Our infantry soon fell back and we opened fire upon the enemy's advancing storming column, composed of, I should think, one brigade
of infantry, one regiment of which were sharpshooters. Our
fire, although very rapid, failed to check them, and on they

came, with bayonets fixed, on our front and right until they
reached the guns, when we, with great difficulty, limbered up
and retired in great haste and confusion, leaving Lieut, Fislar,
one Sergeant, one man, and one gun complete in the enemy's
hands. We then took a position in the rear of the former one,
collected our men and guns expecting another attack, but they
failed to come. Some troops of Genl. Negley's division passed
near me, and I was informed that a new line was being formed
in the rear. Marched with Genl. Negley's division until near
Rossville, when we joined our division. It is, however, my
painful duty to note the death of Capt. A. J. Stevens, as an
artillery officer. He had few equals and no superior. His
only fault was in being too brave and fearless. By his own
personal labor he saved two of his guns on both Saturday and
Sunday, an that, too, when most batteries would have saved
nothing. He fell trying to bring the third piece off by hand.
Long will the artillery of the third division mourn the loss of
this brave and efficient officer and true gentleman. I would
make especial mention of Private Frank Wyman, fourteenth
regiment, Ohio volunteers, as rendering valuable assistance to
the Seventh Indiana battery. On the 20th inst., without his
help, this battery would probably have lost two guns instead
of one.

The battery went into action with 5 officers and 117 men.
Lost, 1 officer, missing; 8 men wounded, two of them missing
and probably dead; one ten-pound Parrott gun.

All of which is most respectfully submitted.

G. R. SWALLOW,
Captain commanding Seventh Indiana Battery.

By an act of the Legislature of Indiana each command engaged on the battlefield of Chickamauga was to have a monument to mark the most dangerous point while in action in that
battle. The commission appointed selected the position held
on Saturday in the Brotherton field for the monument of the
Seventh Indiana battery. This was a very warm and dangerous point, but all members of the battery claim the position
held on Sunday as the most dangerous, and was really the
most disastrous. The design for the monument was furnished
by a member of the battery, with the proper legend. This was
changed for the benefit of some regiment of infantry. When

the battery withdrew from the Brotherton field there were no troops near except Confederates. A regimental monument sets to the right of the battery's position. There were no troops to the right of the battery. The battery was the extreme right of the line. In firing, first direct to the front, the right gun followed the Confederate skirmishers around until it was firing almost direct to the rear. The Confederates were not more than 125 yards away. In withdrawing from this position, in the branch immediately in our rear, a horse to a gun was shot down. The gunners loosed him and got out the gun without the aid of any other troops. In all the maneuvers and actions in this battle the battery came out without the assistance of any other troops except the private spoken of by Capt. Swallow, in his report.

The night of the 23d, about 10 o'clock, the enemy concluded that the Union army was evacuating, and made an attack, but retired after an hour's fighting. General Rosecrans rode along the line, and had a kind word for all. He stated that "we now had a battlefield of our own, and that we came here expecting to have a fight and expected to take Chattanooga, and that we realized both our expectations, and that we had done nobly, and that he had told Genl Hallock that he expected to fight every available man in the army of the south, but not in the army of the Potomac."

The army of the Cumberland is now settling down to camp life, but as they have an enemy around them it is not very pleasant. They are frequently called out at midnight.

October 3 ambulances that had been sent to Chickamauga, returned with wounded men who had been left in the hospitals on the battlefield, and report many of our dead unburied. On October 5, about 10 o'clock a. m , the enemy opened fire on our front. The enemy's signal station on Lookout Mountain overlooks the camp, and they signal the effect of each shot. About noon they opened fire with renewed vigor, and for a time the shot and shell fell quite thick, but doing very little damage. October 12 finds the battery transferred to Baird's division, fourteenth A. C., and associated with the Nineteenth Indiana Battery and Battery I, U.S. Artillery. Capt. Swallow, of the Seventh battery, is Division Chief of Artillery. Everything is quiet in our front, and pickets only three hundred yards apart and on

excellent terms. Bragg's army is undergoing a change and
reorganization. It is reported that Polk's corps was ordered
to make a charge on our works, but not wishing to lead his men
into a slaughter pen, refused to obey. On the 17th the battery
turned over to Battery G, First Missouri Artillery, a twelve
pound gun, and drew one Parrott gun from Capt. Bradley. On
the night of the 20th the battery moved into Fort Negley. Gen.
Rosecrans was superceded by Genl. Thomas today. On the.
21st all hands were busily engaged placing the guns in the
fort.

Rations and forage are scarce. Men are short of food and
horses are dying from starvation, the supplies for the army
having been cut off since the occupation of Chattanooga. The
night of October 29 heavy firing was heard in Lookout valley,
where Genl. Hooker had gone with the twentieth corps. On
November 3 the battery fired a few rounds at the enemy, who
were throwing up works in our front. This put a stop to the
work. On the 4th, being short of men, a detail of thirty-three
was made from the infantry. November 11 a letter was received from Lieut. J. C. Fislar, captured at Chickamauga, and
who is a prisoner at Libby. On the 13th the members of the
battery witnessed the execution of two deserters belonging to
Sheridan's division. On Friday, November 20, while at work
in the fort, orders were received to be ready for action at daylight. These orders were countermanded during the night.
About 2 o'clock, p. m. Monday, Nov. 23, the entire army
moved outside of the works, and at a given signal all the artillery opened fire. Taking advantage of the moment the infantry advanced and took several important positions. The
harmony that had existed between the opposing pickets was at
an end, and lively skirmishing was the order of the hour. The
troops massed in the front and remained on their arms during
the night. Tuesday morning the news came that Genl. Sherman was crossing the river, and was cautiously advancing on
our left. About noon heavy firing of musketry was heard from
Wauhatchie valley, and soon it became evident that Hooker
was endeavoring to arrest Lookout from the enemy. A con-
tinuous line soon came in full view, the enemy falling back,
Hooker's men driving them from behind the rocks. Several
times we would see a flag fall as they came around the point of
the mountain, and some one would sieze it and bear it to the

front. Lieut. O. H. Morgan took his section of two guns and accompanied Harker's brigade to the foot of the mountain and opened fire upon the enemy, dislodging them from behind the rocks, greatly assisting Hooker in gaining the mountain. At dark the artillery ceased firing but the infantry kept up a fusilade until midnight. When daylight came Lookout was in Hooker's possession· At times during the fight the troops engaged were hidden from the view of those in the valley by a cloud hanging below them on the side of the mountain; hence the "fight above the clouds." The enemy having retreated to Mission Ridge, early Wednesday morning the battery was ordered to the center to shell the camps that the enemy were vacating. Heavy fighting could be heard on the left, in front of Sherman. Early in the afternoon Sherman hurled his troops against the strong position of the enemy on Mission Ridge. Three times the enemy charged from their works, but were as many times beaten back. About 3 o'clock, at a signal from a battery on Orchard Knob, a general attack was made, with Sherman on the left, Hooker on the right and Thomas in the center. Thomas, with the army of the Cumberland, was to advance and take possession of the enemy's works at the foot of Mission Ridge, and then halt for further orders, but on carrying the first line of works the men could not be stopped, but on up the ridge they went while fifty pieces of artillery were playing on them. The first point gained on the ridge was near Bragg's headquarters, where a battery was stationed, which was captured and turned on the fleeing enemy, The result of this battle was the complete rout of the enemy, the capture of sixty pieces of artillery and an immense amount of small arms and prisoners. The gun belonging to the battery lost at Chickamauga was here recaptured.

December 25 finds the battery yet in Chattanooga, with just enough horses for two guns, and short of rations, the men amused themselves in different ways, one squad going to the top of Lookout Mountain.

On January 2 the following members of the battery veteranized: George K. Huffman, William H. Hartley, Alex Abbott. William D. Burch. Landa T. Bryant, William Cutsinger, John H. Crane, Samuel C. Colebaker, James Duncan, Hugh Daughty, Robert Gailbraith, James Hord, George W. Hall, Joseph S

Ketchem, Asa Leach, George F. Long, David C. Mann, James
McKain, Levi D. Myers, John F. Martin, Thomas R. Palmer,
Thomas Parsons, Jackson Petro. Lewis Reubright, William A.
Russell, William B. Spurgeon, Wad Salmond and James M.
Thompson.

. February 2 Lieut. Morgan returned, having been absent on
leave for the last thirty days, and the men are receiving full
rations for the first time since the occupancy of Chattanooga.
Among the changes made in the army the battery is placed in
the Third division, Fourteenth A. C.. Genl. Baird commanding.
The Nineteenth and Seventh Indiana batteries and Battery I,
Fourth U. S. Artillery are the batteries associated with this
division, with Capt. Swallow, of the Seventh Indiana, as chief
of artillery.   The brigade with which the battery will operate
is compoaed of the following regiments: Fourth, Tenth and
Eighteenth Kentucky; Tenth and Seventy-fourth Indiana;
Fourteenth and Thirty-eighth Ohio and the Ninety-second Illi-
nois. ···On February 4 Capt. Swallow obtained a leave of absence and started north to remain thirty days.

February 24 finds Lieut. Morgan on his way to Nashville
on business for the battery. On March 12, Lieut. Morgan having returned and is having the battery's equipage overhauled
and all not serviceable is to be condemned and destroyed.
March 19, Capt. Swallow having returned and has been promot-
ed to Major of the tenth cavalry and Lieut. Morgan has re-
ceipted him for the battery. The battery now numbers 161
officers and men.

Lieut. Fislar, captured at Chickamauga, is back from
Libby, having escaped through the noted tunnel. Started to
the front, camping for the night at Rossville. Three o'clock p.
m , of the twentieth found the battery at Ringgold, Ga. April
first Sergt. J. W. Kitzmiller captured at Chickamauga and escaped from Danville, Va, reported today. After almost reaching
the Union lines at Greenville, Tenn., he was recaptured and
taken within a few miles of Danville. He again escaped and
safely made the trip.

Under order issued Nov. 21 thirty-three members of the
battery veteranized and have returned from a leave of absence.
On April 8 the battery was inspected and was honored by a
visit from Major Swallow, of the Tenth Indiana cavalry. On

the 4th, Lieut. Fislar, with the first section, relieved Lieut. Repp from picket. The Seventh was reviewed by Genl. Thomas commander of the army of the Cumberland, after which there was a salute fired in his honor.

On May 5 orders were received to be in readiness at daylight to move to the front. Saturday, May 6, at 2:30 o'clock a. m. reveille was sounded and everything was put in readiness. At 8 o'clock we received orders to take place in the column. Genl. Sherman occupied a position in front of his headquarters, and reviewed his army as it marched by. This was the beginning of the Atlanta campaign.

The column moved on slowly until it reached Tunnel Hill, where it was brought to a halt by the enemy.

The battery, with the division, was held back until the 7th, when it was moved one mile to the front, which brought them in front of Buzzard Roost, where they lay until the 10th, when the whole army was put on the move. Dispatches announcing Grant's victories on the Potomac have just been read to the troops and received with cheers. May 13 finds the army again on the move, taking their positions in front of the enemy. The third division, fourteenth A. C. and its batteries remained quiet until dark, when it advanced, going through Snake creek gap, moving up, as they supposed, on a line with the other forces, but at daylight found that they were some distance in advance, and but a short distance from the enemy's pickets. About 11 o'clock an advance was made and the battery moved forward with the line, when it was brought into action at close range. At daybreak of May 15 they found that the enemy had been busy all night as well as ourselves, preparing for the day's work. The sharp shooters are having it pretty warm. The members of the battery have planted a gun behind a knoll so that they could work it without being exposed to the sharpshooter's fire. Every time the gun was fired a shower of balls would be sent back at them. About 10 o'clock, a move to the right being contemplated, this gun was ordered from its position. In falling back the men became exposed to the enemy's fire, and Sergt. G. K. Hoffman was wounded, and two horses were shot. The move to the right was made with the division. The men worked all night building a fort, and when daylight came found that the enemy had withdrawn, and our forces oc-

32   SEVENTH INDEPENDENT BATTERY,

cupied Resacca. The enemy, in their retreat, burned the
bridge ver the Coosa river. May 17, at 1 o'clock a. m , reveille
was sounded, and at 3 o'clock a m. the battery was on the
move. After a long and fatigueing march we went into camp
three miles south of Calhoun. On the 19th we moved on to
Cassville, where we remained until the 23d, when the march
was again taken up, At 9 o'clock a m. we crossed the river at
a ford. After marching about ten miles we went into camp at
Island creek, where there was an abundance of fresh water and
forage, a fine country and beautiful homes, but all deserted.

On the 24th, at noon, the battery, with the third brigade,
marched a few miles, was turned about and sent back into
camp. The cause was said to be fear that the wagon train
would be raided. The battery remained in camp until the
morning of the 26, when the command received orders to move
to the front. After a twelve miles march we went into camp
in Burnt Hickory valley. As the battery was located in a nice
shady spot the men were greatly dissatisfied when Genl. Baird
ordered the Captain to change his camp to an open field, but on
the 27th the officers changed to a pleasant spot in the woods,
May 28, at noon, we moved to the front, and stopped three
miles from Dallas, returning the next day to Burnt Hickory,
and camped on the Marietta road twenty-one miles from that
place. We remained in camp until June 1, when orders were
received to move to the front   Lieut Repp's section remained
with Genl. Turchin. The command marched through a deso-
late mountainous country, and found many families in destitute
circumstances, who were favored with donations of bacon and
crackers, which were gratefully received. After marching ten
miles the battery bivouacked in the rear of the division.

On June 2 there was a general movement of forces to the
left. The battery took a position on a hill behind works that
had been occupied by Johnson's divison. During the day the
forces were drenched by a very hard storm. The Union lines
were advanced and a new line of works was thrown up. Early
in the morning of June 3 the battery moved out to the advance,
where the time was spent shelling the enemy's skirmishers, and
the lines advanced still further without much serious loss. The
4th was also put in shelling the enemy from houses, and re-
pelling several attempted advances of the enemy. Gener-

als'Sherman, Thomas and Palmer were at the battery several
times during the day.   At night the enemy kept up a rattling
fire that several times looked serious, but it proved only feints
to cover their retreat.   After a tiresome delay on the 6th the
battery finally got started and marched in rear of Davis' division. About dark, after marching fourteen miles "the powers
that be" ascertained that they were on the wrong road.   They
had to go by by-ways, over hills, and through hollows until
midnight, to get righted.   They brought up near Acworth,
where they rested three days, moving on the 10th with our division in the advance.   After passing Big Shanty skirmishing
commenced and two guns of the battery were placed on the
line and shelled Pine Mt., but could receive no reponse.   We
could see quite a force at work on rifle pits. All the men were
up most of the night throwing up works, part of the time during a hard rain   The guns were in position on the morning of
the 11th, but very little firing was done during the day. Genl.
Thomas was near the battery's position all day.   Late in the
evening the Union lines were advanced.   All day of the 12th
it rained, and the army remained quiet.   On June 14 the lines
were advanced half a mile.   At daylight of the 16th we left the
old position and took a new one, and during the day fired a
number of shells at the enemy.   The men were at work all
night erecting a fort, and as it was on the skirmish line great
care had to be used about exposing ourselves.   During the
night the enemy evacu'ted a portion of their works.   A heavy
rain fell all day of the 18th.   About noon the lines advanced
and the enemy was found strongly entrenched.   The battery
started with the corps on the Marietta road, and brought up in
front of Kenesaw mountain, where a number of shells were
fired at the works on the side of the mountain.   In the afternoon of the 23d we moved on the line where, while strengthening
the works, A. D. Broady was severely wounded in the head, by
a piece of snell, and John Gibbons and Milton Boyd slightly
wounded by balls.   The battery had been under very heavy
firing.   In action here a shot from the battery closed the muz-
zle of a brass piece of the enemy, rendering it useless.   Also a
shot from the battery exploded a caisson of the enemy.   This
information was obtained from two Confederates who were
manning the gun, and deserted at Marietta, June 28.   The battery has been in front of Kenesaw eight days—a long time to

be under fire. By order all the artillery on the line were to
commence firing at 8 o'clock, a. m., when a general charge
would be made. At the appointed time all the batteries commenced firing, and when they stopped the infantry advanced
from the works and charged along the entire line, but were repulsed with great loss. A truce was granted for
the purpose of giving each side an opportunity to bury their
dead.

On the 29th several shots were fired, as also every day until
the night of July 1, when the battery was relieved by one of
Genl. Osterhaus' batteries. The Seventh reported to its divis--
ion and marched until 2 o'clock a. m., and after two hours' rest
was hurried out and took a position near a division on a hill,
commanding the enemy's line   On the morning of July 3 orders
were received to prepare to move immediately. It was soon
known that the enemy had flown. The fourteenth corps
marched through Marietta, pushing the enemy very close. The
battery camped two miles south of Marietta. July 4 the command laid in camp. This was the first days' real rest they had
for two weeks.

On July 5th the army was on the move. The division to
which the battery was attached was in the advance, which occasionally brought us into action. About noon, by order of
Genl. Baird, two guns were placed on a high hill, overlooking
Vining Station and commanding the country south of the Chattahoochee river. From here the battery shelled the enemy's
cavalry. They were pushed so hard that they left their pon-
toons in the Union forces' possession. Before dark the battery
withdrew and went into camp, where they remained four days.
The night of the 9th works were thrown up, which the battery
occupied.

Early the morning of the 16th Capt. Morgan and Lieut.
Fislar left for Marietta for the purpose of exchanging three
Parrott guns for three Rodman guns. The bands of each army
exchanged patriotic airs, which were received with cheers from
each side. We remained in this position until the 18th, when
about noon, the battery crossed the river and camped about
three miles south. Here was a large cotton mill belonging to
an Englishman who claimed protection under the English flag.
(Probably he went to England after it.) The mill was burned,

and a great number of operators thrown out, who were sent north. The morning of the 19th, at 7 o'clock, the battery was ordered out, and after a march of two miles found the enemy in a strong position at Peach Tree creek. Lieut, Fislar put one gun in position and kept up quite a fire for some time. Capt. Morgan moved three guns forward, and the men threw up light works for protection against sharpshooters. Toward evening Genl. Davis crossed the creek and made a severe fight. The battery shelled in his advance. Lost here by wound, Private I. L. Ramp. On the 20th had quite a fight in advancing the lines. The morning of July 22 news passed along the line that the enemy was evacuating Atlanta. The whole army was on the move, each corps commander seemingly anxious to have the honor of being first to enter the city. They had gone but a short distance when the enemy was found in force, and heavy fighting began to our left. Here is where Genl. McPherson fell. After the fight the fourteenth corps, to which the battery belonged, moved to within two miles of the city. The battery was placed in position to the north of the city, and about one and one-fourth miles from the enemy's heavy line. The night of the 22d was spent in throwing up works. We expected an attack on the 23d, but were not molested.

On Sunday, the 24th, the heavy guns of the army dropped shell in the city at intervals of five minutes during the day. The battery amused itself with its Rodman guns in stopping details of the enemy from working on their line. This firing was kept up from day to day until the 30th, when in the afternoon the enemy opened on the battery with a sixty-four pounder, the shell bursting, scattering fragments among the tents like hail. During the day two of the battery horses were killed. On Sunday, 31st, several shots were fired at a regiment going through their Sunday inspection. August 1, at night, orders were given to fire ten rounds to each gun on the city. As this order was issued to every battery that could reach the city the bombardment was general and shell fell in the city from all parts of the line. There was a general move of the army to the right. The morning of August 4 the fourteenth corps moved three miles to the right, but the battery did not move from its position until about dark, and after going a short distance were ordered into camp by Genl. Sherman, to await until morning and then report to the corps. As the roads were

in a very bad condition and it was raining hard they were very
glad to obey the General's order. The next morning the march
was taken up. We had went about two miles when a detail
commenced building a fort on a line with the reserve pickets.
During the afternoon several of the enemy's pickets were captured, and the battery had quite an artillery duel with the enemy's batteries. On the 5th, when the picket lines were but a
short distance apart, the third division of the fourteenth corps
made a charge and captured the entire line. The battery was
in action at this time and did good service in supporting the
charge. From the 5th to the 10th the battery was firing occasionally at whatever showed up, or where they thought they
could dislodge a sharpshooter. On the night of the 10th the
enemy put up a fort about eight hundred yards to our front.
The battery fired a few shots to get the range, and when the
gunners had it every shot was put in the embrasures, and the
enemy was soon driven out of their works. Occasional firing
was kept up until the 13th, when in the afternoon the enemy's
skirmish line, at a given signal, threw down their arms and
came into the Union lines in a body. The enemy's batteries
opened upon them, but the Union force gave them protection
and welcomed them in. The battery had a position for their
protection. During the night the battery was brought into action to prevent the enemy from advancing and planting their
batteries nearer the Union lines.

The morning of the 18th orders were received to be ready
to move at a moment's notice. Suspicious movements were reported in the enemy's camp. During the night troops were
moving to our rear and right, and the 19th finds the brigade
and battery in full charge of the whole division's front. The
enemy, however, are not aware of our weakness, and have remained inactive. They were inactive until Sunday, 21. During
the morning the enemy opened with a battery on the Union line
and made it pretty warm in the neighborhood of the Seventh
battery for a while. About noon everything became quiet, and
the enemy, as well as ourselves, seemed to enjoy the cessation
of hostilities. The two brigades of the division returned and
took their place on the line, and nothing but occasional firing
and brushes between the skirmishers transpiring until about 9
o'clock p. m. of the 26th, when the division commenced to retire, leaving a strong picket line which kept up a strong fusi-

lade to conceal the withdrawal. The enemy evidently heard them, as they opened fire, which the battery returned with a few rounds, then quietly took its place in the column. The wagons belonging to the battery had been on a foraging expedition and returned just in time to save the battery's property, which otherwise would have fallen into the hands of the enemy. After an all night's march the battery went into camp several miles to the right. On the 27th the battery moved out at 5 o'clock, without breakfast, and after a three mile march went into camp in front of corps headquarters. The morning of the 28th, at 3 o'clock reveille was sounded, and at 5 o'clock we moved to the right until we reached the Montgomery and Atlanta railroad, when the command bivouacked for the night. While in camp here the battery was called out to shell the enemy's cavalry. Nothing occurred on the 29th and 30th except, on the latter day a short march. While at breakfast on the 31st orders were received to move out with Walker's brigade, to shell the enemy's wagon train, which was done in a handsome manner, completely demoralizing both the drivers and teams.

On September 1 the Third division, Fourteenth corps, moved to the right and struck the enemy near Jonesboro, Ga. After the first and second brigades had several times charged the enemy and were repulsed, the third brigade, charged the works and captured the Eighth and Nineteenth Arkansas regiments and Swett's battery. The battery was in position but did no firing. We camped that night on the battlefield. On the 2nd the battery moved into Jonesboro, and remained until the 6th, when they moved out as the enemy's skirmishers entered. The battery moved a short distance and went into camp. The forces started for Atlanta on the 7th, leaving Lieut. Fislar's section with the rear guard. We stopped for the night at Rough & Ready. On the 8th the battery moved on to one mile of Atlanta, where it camped.

REPORT OF CAPT. O. H. MORGAN, ON THE ATLANTA
CAMPAIGN.

HEADQUARTERS SEVENTH INDIANA BATTERY, }
JONESBOROUGH, GA , September 6, 1864.   }

Major: I have the honor to transmit you the following report of the operations of the Seventh Indiana Battery in this
campaign:

At 8 o'clock on the morning of May 6, 1864, the battery
moved out from Ringgold, Ga·, with the Third Division, Fourteenth Army Corps, on the Dalton road, and early in the afternoon camped near Tunnel Hill. From the 7th to 12th nothing
of note occurred except a few changes of camp. May 12,
moved to the right, and passing through Snake Creek Gap,
camped after a march of twenty miles. May 14, in obedience
to your orders, four guns were placed on the line in front of
the regular brigade, First Division, Fourteenth Army Corps.
Two guns had an enfilading fire on the enemy, to the left, and
one section aided in silencing two guns in front. Lieutenant
Pound and section was sent per order of Captain Estep, division chief of artillery, half a mile to the left, and took position
on a commanding ridge, directing his fire mainly at a rebel
battery in his front. During the night of the 14th the enemy
was heard erecting works, but, expecting orders to change position, no preparations were made for defense until just before
daylight. No orders coming I moved Lieutenant Repp's section
400 yards to the left, and placed Lieutenant Fislar's section be·
hind a little crest, and employed what little time we had before
day in putting up a protection to shield the gunners. It was
found almost impossible to work the guns on account of the
nearness to the enemy's sharpshooters, but a random fire was
kept up until we were relieved. Late in the forenoon Captain
Estep ordered me to withdraw, which was done as speedily as
possible. For seventy-five yards Lieutenant Fislar's section
was exposed to a flank fire of musketry, but the move was so
unexpected that most of the men were under cover before the

heaviest fire was opened. Sergeant Hoffman was severely wounded and two horses shot in this operation. Lieutenants Repp and Pound came out with their sections and the battery moved with the division several miles to the right, and one section relieved two guns of some Iowa battery, and fired several shots at the rebel works, but elicited no reply. On the 16th marched and crossed the Coosa river at Resaca at midnight, and parked for the men to breakfast while the division was coming up; passed through Calhoun and camped for the night three miles south. On the 19th camped near Cassville, where we remained until the 23rd, when we took up the route of march, fording the Etowa at Island Ford, and after ten miles march, camped on Island Creek; two days passed without a move. Marched to Burnt Hickory valley on the 26th. At noon on the 28th moved four miles to the front, returning next day to Burnt Hickory. June 1, reporting Lieutenant Repp's section to General Turchin, who remained as train guard, marched ten miles to the front. June 3, advanced the battery to the line of Col. Este's brigade, and during this and the succeeding day kept up a desultory fire on the rebel skirmishers, driving them from houses, and in conjunction with the Nineteenth Indiana battery repelled several attempted advances of the enemy. Marched on the 6th and camped near Acworth. Rested three days and moved on the 10th, and finding the enemy on Pine Mountain one section was put in position per order of General Baird. and during this and the succeeding day shelled the mountain. June 11, withdrew from this position and remained quiet until the 15th when we advanced several miles. and that night built works on our division line and put the battery in position. Early in the morning of the 16th General Palmer ordered the woods and valley in my front to be shelled, and on the afternoon of that day General Thomas sent orders to open a vigorous fire on a nest of sharpshooters that prevented an advance, which was accordingly done; during the night of the 16th, threw up an advanced work, and the next day occupying it, assisted our troops to advance by dislodging their skirmishers. Late in the afternoon of the 18th I got two guns into position on the right of Battery 1, First Ohio Artillery, and opened fire on a rebel fort 1,300 yards distant, which was feebly replied to. Moved forward on the 19th, and in the afternoon took position in front of Kenesaw mountain, by order of General Palmer.

The side of the mountain occupied by sharpshooters was
shelled, and late in the day I directed the fire on a battery off
to our right. During the next two days fired occassional shots,
and in the afternoon of the 23d moved into position on the line
occupied by the Third Brigade, Third Division, Fourteenth
Army corps, in front of Little Kenesaw Mountain. I immediately commenced strengthening the works, and while so occupied was much annoyed by an enfilade fire from a rebel battery.
Early in the forenoon of the next day the enemy's batteries on
the mountain and along the line concentrated a terrific fire on
the batteries in front of the Third Division, and for an hour
the cannonading was very heavy. My bugler, Asa D. Broody,
was here severely wounded in the head by a piece of shell, and
Privates Gibbons and Boyd slightly hurt by bullets. Our division was relieved on the night of the 25th by the Fifteenth Army
corps, and on the morning of the 26th General McPherson directed me to open a heavy fire on the batteries in range previous
to a charge his corps would make at 8 o'clock. His order was
obeyed until the advance of his line made it unsafe to fire. Remained in this position, firing more or less every day, until I
was relieved on the night of July 1, by one of General Osterhaus' batteries, when I reported back to my division, and was
put in position at daylight by Captain Estep. Exchanged a
number of shots during the day with the enemy. Marched on
the 3d and camped two miles south of Marietta. July 5, moved
again, and towards noon General Baird ordered my battery up
the mountain overlooking Vining's Station, and here we shelled
the rear guard of the enemy just crossing the Chattahoochee.
Before dark withdrew and went into camp, where we remained
four days. Built works on the night of the 9th, but, the enemy
evacuating, moved into position commanding the fort. July 18
crossed the Chattahoochee and camped four miles south.
Moved at 7 o'clock on the morning of the 19th, and after two
miles march found the enemy posted just across Peach Tree
creek. In accordance with your order, took position on a
ridge near the skirmish line, and kept up a fire until dark.
Private Ramp was severely wounded by a musket ball. Marched
July 22 and took position within two miles of Atlanta, where
we remained twelve days. Fired at intervals during this per-
iod, directing most of our shots at the city and the rebel works
in front. August 4, moved three miles to the right, and, by

your order, took position in front of Genl. Baird's division, from which point we did not open until the 6th. Made several demonstrations at times, by order of General Baird. Sergeant Kitzmiller, Corporal McPheeters, and Privates Watson and Mann were wounded in this position on the 7th, two of them by shells and two by musketry. Remained here until the night of the 26th, when we withdrew under the fire of the rebel batteries, and marched several miles to the right. From the 27th to the evening of the 30th short marches were made, and nothing of interest occurred. On the morning of the 31st moved out to the line with Colonel Walker's brigade, Third Division, and threw a number of shells at a large rebel wagon train, which soon changed its course, and passed out of view. September 1 moved forward with General Baird's division, and, nearing the battle-field, was halted by Major Lowrie, assistant adjutant-general Third Division, and held ourselves in readiness to move until after dark, when we went into camp for the night, by order of Major Lowrie. September 2, moved into Jonesborough, where we are now located.

I take pleasure in according to the officers and men of my command much credit for their excellent conduct during this arduous and memorable campaign.

Effective force of Battery May 5, 1864 .... 148 men.
Effective force of Battery Sept. 5, 1864....... 110 men.
Rounds of ammunition expended on campaign. 6,083.

Very respectfully, your obedient Servant,

O. H. MORGAN,

Captain, commanding Seventh Indiana Battery.

MAJ. CHARLES HOUGHTALING,
Chief of Artillery, Fourteenth Army Corps.

On October 2d the Captain turned over two guns and sixteen horses to the fifth Wisconsin battery, which moved on the third with the corps, (Fourteenth), after Hood. The Captain received orders on the eighth from Genl. Bowman to draw two guns for temporary use, which was done, and in the afternoon they were placed in charge of Lieut. Masterson, who camped with his new section a few rods north of the city. Lieut. Repp section was placed a short distance to our left.

On October 18 by Genl. Slocum's order, the Captain drew

six twenty pound Parrott guns and placed them in a fort on the inner line of the works. The Captain left on the twenty-ninth of October on a leave of twenty days, returning on November seventeenth and finding the battery ready to go to Chattanooga to prepare to go to Indianapolis, to be mustered out, having turned over everything to the Quartermaster and leaving the following recruits and veterans at Chattanooga, to be consolidated with those of the Eighth Indiana Battery under the name of the Seventh reorganized:

Allen Alloway, Mark Arnold, Henderson Alexander, Alex Abbott, John Bonifacine, John W. Beatty. Freeman T. Beymer. William D. Burch, Sylvester Clark, Alfred Clark, William D. Cochrane, William H. Clark, Robert A. Craigg. George Cave, John H. Crane, William Cutsinger, Samuel C. Colebaker, Phineas DeFord, James Duncan, Hugh Daugherty, Andrew Ewing, Eph B. Fletcher, William A. Fletcher, Dennis Grissamore, John Gibbons. John Geisler, Robert Gailbraith, J. Thos. Hunter, Alfred D. Hauger, Joseph B. Howard, Franklin Holwick, John Heinke. Philip Hulen, Abner Hulen, John Hopson, James Hord, George W. Hall, Adam Jones, William A. Johns, John S. Johns, Joseph S. Ketcham, William H. Landers, Newton Luck, George W. Luck, Francis D. Littlejohn, Asa Leach, George F. Long. Joseph A. McCoskey, William H. McPheeters, William H. McCoskey, David C. Mann, Levi D. Myers, James McKain, John F. Martin, Joseph Pound, William Powers, Thos. Parsons, Jackson Petro, Robert Richardson, James Reed, Jas. J. Roberts, John W. Russell, William H. Ray, William A. Russell, Lewis Reubright, William H. Sanders, Oliver R. Smith, Dawson Shull, John M Stark, Fred Schwam, James Slaughter, Soloman Schroyer, Thomas Simpson, Ward Salmond, William H. Spurgeon, William Trinkle. Darling Thomerson, Charles A. Thomerson, Peter Tuscan, Noah W. Tryon, Joseph M. Thompson, Samuel Vickers, Howard Vickers, David Watts, George W. Watson, Fleming Wingler. Lemuel Weeks, Charles H. Watson, Joseph H. Young, Jerome Young, David York, Daniel Zink.

On the twentieth of November those whose time would expire on the seventh of December, started for the North. The men were given arms to defend themselves with, as the trains had frequently been attacked. Arriving at Indianapolis where they remainded several days and on the seventh day of December 1864, the following officers and men were mustered out. Otho H. Morgan, Captian; George M. Repp. George C. Masterson, John C. Fislar, Columbus S, Pound, Lieutenants.

James E. Anderson, Fenton Butterfield, William Boyd. John E. Bowman, John W. Boyd, Asa D. Broady, Newton Bledsoe, Sterling Carter, Andrew M. Carmichael, Edmond H. Coles, William Coman, John Duff, Edwin S. Dills, Jacob Garris, Chrispen S. Goen. William F. Gibbson, Jacob W. Harris, John Heller, Greenbury Huff, Mahlon Johnson, Adam Johnson, John M. Kemp, John Kitzmiller, Edgar R. Murphy, D. Newton McKee, Cyrus Martin, Jacob McConnelly, Edward McIntosh, Solomon McIntosh, Abner Mitchem, Nehemiah Mitchem, Tillman A. Moore, William S. Moore, Ithamer C. Owens, George Paul Benj. F. Roberts, Lewis J. Ramsey, Abram S. Reed, Jasper Reno, John Short, John E. Scott, Joseph E. Smallwood, Tillman C. Stewart, Henry Smallwood, Henry A. Steinbarger, William A. Taylor, Michal W. Wilson, Edgar T. White, David A. Welch, Miles B. Young.

List of losses from all causes: Captains, S. J. Harris, and George R. Swallow; Lieutenants F. W. Buckmar, John J. Hawes and Lewis B. Leonard; Enlisted men, Abner Cook, Henry W. Hackley, Jacob Funderburg, John P. Allen, Stephen S. Batt, George W. Bealman, Robert O. Bosley, John Bush, Joel H. Crum, Elihu Dixon, Thomas J. Fulk. Charles Hickling, Abner E Haines, Fred Helmohl, Isaac Ketchem, James H. McCroskey, Thomas McQuilkin, Thomas R Palmer. Andrew Reubright. John Reynolds, Christ Ritline, James A. Risley, James Smallwood, William A. Thurston, Theadore Wiles, Parker Alexander. John D. Bruner, Francis J. Dean, Henry M. Engleman, Elisha Gibson, John M. Watson, Jacob Launis, Murdock McGregory. Charles Munwarren, Cornelius McCarty, Josiah L. Ramp. Eakin J. Roberts, James Reed, Edward Starr, Hiram Tryon, Daniel Zink, Charles Brash, George Dunlap, Isaac Funderburg. John Garr, George F. Lindley, George W. May, Charles May, Jesse Pound, Jason A. Rogers, Charles Williams, James Atkins, Henry Copeland, Hardin Woole, John Woole, R. Willbanks.

As we talk over the trials and troubles, the pleasures and hardships of a three years' military life, we must not forget

those who fell in action. As General Thomas said, "Their
graves mark the spot where they went down amid the roar of
battle, dotting field and hillside, or lie beneath the spreading
boughs of the trees along our road. They will, in future days,
serve as finger boards to point to the traveler the marches of
our victorious columns."

The camp life of '61 and '62 at Green River, and the march
to Bacon Creek and Elizabethtown, then the return, and on to
Nashville, were a continuation of rains, and the roads were in a
terrible condition. Also the marches from Nashville to Stone
River, from Murfreesboro to Manchester, and from Chattanooga to Atlanta were anything but comfortable. On the Atlanta
campaign, which consumed one hundred and twenty-five days
from the time the battery left Ringgold until it arrived at Atlanta, but very few days passed that it was not in action, and
during that time there were nineteen days of rain. While on
Pumpkin Vine creek and near New Hope there were several
severe thunder storms that seemed would deluge the whole
army. All these, and what is herein written, will te remembered by those who participated, and they will be the means of
reviving the past. As you read it will bring to your mind in-
stances of which you have forgotten.

We have here endeavored to give a true unexaggerated history of the marches and trials of the Seventh battery. Taking
all the hardships. as each one well knows, would be impossible
to describe, and to undertake to give each individuals service,
would be impossible, therefore it is given as a battery and hope
that each member will be contented with the honor he has received as a member of that battery. The .battery has been
honored by that best of all war Governors, O. P. Morton, by
retaining its original number, as you remember that when the
original members left Chattanooga, for muster out, the veterans
and the recruits were consolidated. with those of the Eight Indiana Battery. under the title of the Seventh battery reorganized. On the fifth day of April, 1865, the remnant of the
Fifth battery was transferred to this reorganized Seventh battery and mustered out, July 20, 1865. as the Seventh battery.

We now close this and hope that the seven years of labor

in attaining what is here recorded, will be appreciated by our comrads.

Your most obediently,

O. H. MORGAN,
E. R. MURPHY.

Committee appointed December 31, 1891.

NOTES.

The title, "Seventh Independent Battery, Indiana Light Artillery," is the nom de plume in which the battery started out. It was supposed there would be regimental organization, but the Government refused to recognize any such organization among the volunteer troops, so the battery dropped a portion of her title, and it was thereafter called the Seventh Battery, Indiana Light Artillery.

On page 10, Aug. 17, Decard should be Decherd. W. L. Smith should be W. S. Smith.

On page 13, in the battle of Dobbins' ford, the Thirty fifth Indiana Battery should read Thirty-fifth Indiana Regiment and Seventh Indiana Battery.

On page 19, Capt. Drewry should read Drury.

On page 23, line 20, the road should read Chattanooga and Lafayette pike.

On page 24 the Twenty-first Division should read Third Brigade, Third Division, Twenty-first Corps.

www.ingramcontent.com/pod-product-compliance
Lightning Source LLC
Chambersburg PA
CBHW021431090426
42739CB00009B/1453